Pope Francis

Barbara Kramer

NATIONAL GEOGRAPHIC
Washington, D.C.

For my mother, who encouraged me to write —B. K.

Published by the National Geographic Society, Washington, D.C. 20036.

Trade paperback ISBN: 978-1-4263-2253-2
Reinforced library binding ISBN: 978-1-4263-2254-9

Editor: Shelby Alinsky
Art Director: Callie Broaddus
Editorial: Snapdragon Books
Designer: YAY! Design
Photo Editor: Lori Epstein
Rights Clearance: Michael Cassady and Mari Robinson
Manufacturing Manager: Rachel Faulise
Production Assistant: Sanjida Rashid

The author and publisher gratefully acknowledge the expert content review of this book by Jean-Pierre Isbouts, D.Litt., humanities scholar and professor at Fielding Graduate University, and the literacy review of this book by Mariam Jean Dreher, professor of reading education, University of Maryland, College Park.

Photo Credits

CO: Corbis; GI: Getty Images
Cover, WENN US/Alamy; (background), WDG Photo/Shutterstock; 1, 3, 4, 5, Dave Yoder/National Geographic Society; 6, age fotostock/Alamy; 7, NG Maps; 8 (UP), Filippo Fiorini/Demotix/CO; 8 (LO), ANSA/ANS/CO; 9 (UP and LO), Filippo Fiorini/Demotix/CO; 10, Jesuit General Curi/GI; 11, Piko Press/Splash New/CO; 12 (UP), API/GAMMA/Gamma-Rapho/GI; 12 (LO), Alessandro Bianchi/Reuters; 13, Tarker/CO; 14 (UP), GDA/AP Images; 14 (LO), Yara Nardi/Reuters; 15 (UP), epa/Rolling Stone/Handout/Alamy; 15 (CTR), NG Maps; 15 (LO), Stefano Rellandini/Reuters/CO; 16, El Salvador School/AP Images; 17, El Salvador School/AP Images; 18, Handout/Reuters; 19 (UP), AP Images; 19 (LO), Douglas Engle/CO; 20 (UP), Jules_Kitano/Shutterstock; 20 (CTR), Franco Origlia/GI; 20 (LO), Alejandro Pagni/AFP/GI; 21 (UP), L'Osservatore Romano/AP Images; 21 (CTR UP), Olivier Morin/AFP/GI; 21 (CTR LO and LO), catwalker/Shutterstock; 22, Enrique Marcarian/Reuters; 23 (UP), Pablo Leguizamon/AP Images; 23 (LO), Dave Yoder/National Geographic Society; 24, Buenos Aires Archbishop Office/AP Images; 25, Kay Nietfeld/dpa/CO; 26, Macdiarmid/GI; 27 (INSET), Dave Yoder/National Geographic Society; 27, Osservatore Romano/AFP/GI; 28–29, Dave Yoder/National Geographic Society; 30 (LE), Juan Mabromata/AFP/GI; 30 (RT), Spencer Plat/GI; 31 (UP LE), Grupo44/LatinContent/GI; 31 (UP RT), Alejandro Pagni/AFP/GI; 31 (LO LE), Piko Press/Splash News/CO; 31 (LO RT), franck-reporter/iStockphoto; 32 (UP LE), AP Images; 32 (UP RT), Alessandra Benedetti/CO; 32 (LO LE), El Salvador School/AP Images; 32 (LO RT), Piko Press/Splash News/CO; top border of pages (throughout), Nataleana/Shutterstock; vocabulary box art, andromina/Shutterstock

National Geographic supports K–12 educators with ELA Common Core Resources. Visit natgeoed.org/commoncore for more information.

Printed in the United States of America
15/WOR/1

Table of Contents

Who Is Pope Francis?   4

The Future Pope   6

Choosing a Path   10

Pope Francis's Cool Firsts   14

Helping Others   16

6 Fun Facts About Pope Francis   20

One of the People   22

A New Pope   26

What in the World?   30

Glossary   32

Who Is Pope Francis?

Pope Francis is the leader of the Roman Catholic Church. He lives in Vatican City in Rome. That is the home of the Catholic Church. There have been many popes, or leaders of the church, over the years. Pope Francis became the pope in 2013.

inside St. Peter's Cathedral in Vatican City

People from all over the world look up to Pope Francis.

The Future Pope

Francis was the name he chose when he became pope. Until then, he was Jorge Mario Bergoglio (HOR-hay MA-ree-o bear-GO-lee-o).

Buenos Aires, Argentina

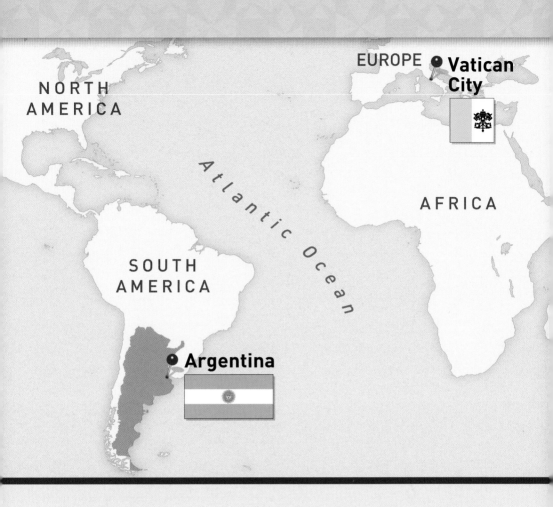

Bergoglio was born on December 17, 1936. He grew up in Buenos Aires (BWAY-nus I-reez). That is the capital city of Argentina (are-jen-TEE-na).

Bergoglio was the oldest of five children. As a boy, he played soccer and basketball with his friends. He liked to read, too.

Bergoglio is on the left with his brother Oscar.

Bergoglio's father, Mario, and his grandmother, Rosa

His Grandmother Rosa taught him to pray. On Sundays, he went to church with his family.

Bergoglio's elementary school, Pedro Cervio, in Buenos Aires

Bergoglio's elementary school class in 1943. He is in the bottom right corner.

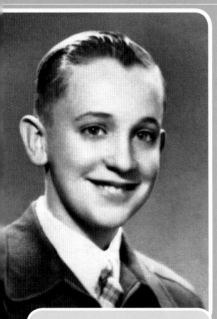

Bergoglio as a young man

Bergoglio liked to learn about his faith and the church. He was 17 years old when he first thought about becoming a priest (preest). He wanted to help people learn more about the church.

When he was 19 years old, he entered a seminary (SEM-uh-ner-ee). There he studied to become a priest.

Words to Know

PRIEST: a person who serves God and may also be the minister of a church

SEMINARY: a school for future priests

seminary in Villa Devoto in Buenos Aires, Argentina

Bergoglio with his parents and four siblings. Bergoglio is in the top center, dressed as a priest.

In His Own Words

"Life is a journey."

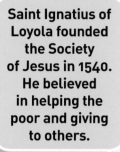

Saint Ignatius of Loyola founded the Society of Jesus in 1540. He believed in helping the poor and giving to others.

Bergoglio wanted to be part of a special group of priests. That group is called the Society of Jesus. Its members are known as Jesuits (JEH-zoo-its). In 1958, Bergoglio joined the society.

Pope Francis's Cool Firsts

Pope Francis was the first to do a lot of things. Did you know these "firsts"?

He is the first pope from the group of priests known as Jesuits.

He is the first pope to pose for "selfies."

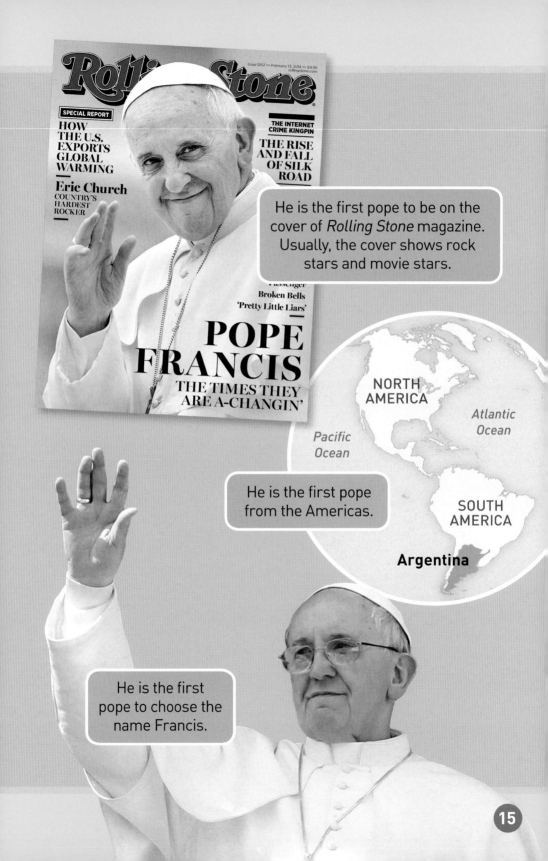

He is the first pope to be on the cover of *Rolling Stone* magazine. Usually, the cover shows rock stars and movie stars.

He is the first pope from the Americas.

He is the first pope to choose the name Francis.

Helping Others

In His Own Words

"Help each other always."

Bergoglio was 33 years old when he became a priest.

Jesuit priests believe in helping the poor. They do not spend much money on themselves. They live simply and give to others. That is what Bergoglio wanted to do.

He studied for many years. He also worked as a teacher. In 1969, he became a priest.

This photo from 1973 shows Bergoglio (on the left) as a priest.

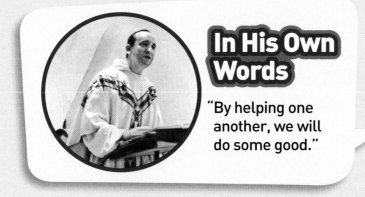

"By helping one another, we will do some good."

Bergoglio became a leader in the church. In 1992, he became a bishop in Buenos Aires. His job was to help priests in the city. Six years later, Bergoglio was named archbishop. That meant he was in charge of an even larger area.

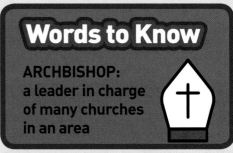

Words to Know

ARCHBISHOP: a leader in charge of many churches in an area

Bergoglio holds a Mass, or church service, in Argentina in 2000.

Bergoglio often worked to help people in the poorest areas of Buenos Aires.

6 FUN FACTS
About Pope Francis

1
BIENVENIDOS A LA REPUBLICA ARGENTINA

Jorge is the Spanish word for George. Spanish is the language of Argentina.

Bergoglio is an excellent cook. His mother taught him.

2

3

Bergoglio has been a lifelong soccer fan. His favorite team is San Lorenzo of Buenos Aires.

For his 77th birthday, Pope Francis invited a group of homeless men and a dog to join him for breakfast.

4

5

Pope Francis gets up early to pray for two hours before beginning his day.

As a young man, Pope Francis collected stamps. Now there are postage stamps with his face on them.

6

Brasil 2013 R$1,80

JMJ RIO2013

Fernando Lopes

do Papa Francisco ao Brasil

CITTÀ DEL VATICANO

ANNO I S.P. MMXIII

FRANCISCVS PP.

One of the People

When Bergoglio became archbishop, there was a large home with servants where he could live. Bergoglio said it was too fancy. He moved into a small apartment instead.

Bergoglio used to hold Mass in this church in a poor neighborhood in Buenos Aires. In this photo, the people are celebrating Bergoglio being named pope.

Bergoglio riding the subway in 2008

In His Own Words

"My people are poor and I am one of them."

He also said no to using a special car with his own driver. He rode the bus or took the subway.

Pope John Paul II and Bergoglio on the day Bergoglio was made a cardinal

In 2001, Pope John Paul II made Bergoglio a cardinal. Cardinals are church leaders who help the pope.

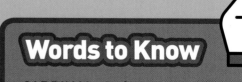

Words to Know

CARDINAL: An important leader in the Roman Catholic Church. A cardinal serves under the pope.

Pope Benedict XVI became pope in 2005. Eight years later, he said he could no longer be pope. He was getting old and was not strong enough.

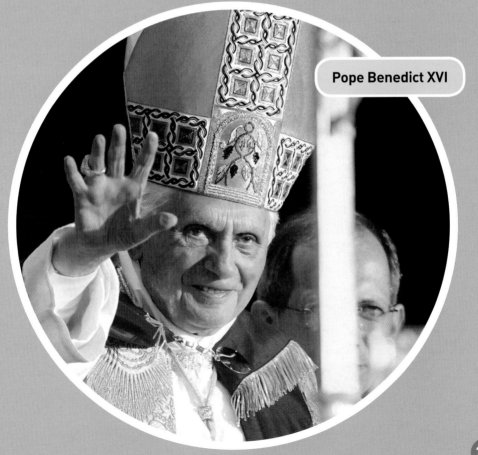

Pope Benedict XVI

A New Pope

In March 2013, many cardinals met in Vatican City. Bergoglio was one of them. The cardinals would choose one of themselves as the new pope.

They spent two days talking about who it would be. Finally, they picked Bergoglio. He chose the name Pope Francis.

In His Own Words

"And now, we take up this journey ... of fraternity, of love, of trust among us."

Pope Francis lives simply. It is what he has always done. He helps the poor and all people who have hard lives. He also spends time meeting the people he serves. People like that about him. Some call him "the people's pope."

1936
Born on
December 17

1955
Begins studies
at a seminary

1969
Becomes a
priest

28

1998

Named
Archbishop of
Buenos Aires

2001

Becomes a
cardinal

2013

Chosen to
be the pope

What in the World?

These pictures show items in Pope Francis's life. Use the hints to figure out what's in the pictures. Answers are on page 31.

1

2

HINT: a game Pope Francis loves to watch

HINT: Pope Francis collected these as a kid.

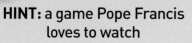

Word Bank

church   selfie   stamps   seminary   subway   soccer

3

4

HINT: Pope Francis went here with his family on Sundays.

HINT: Pope Francis rode this in Buenos Aires.

5

6

HINT: Pope Francis studied here to become a priest.

HINT: Pope Francis is the first pope to pose for one.

Answers: 1. soccer, 2. stamps, 3. church, 4. subway, 5. seminary, 6. selfie

ARCHBISHOP: a leader in charge of many churches in an area

CARDINAL: An important leader in the Roman Catholic Church. A cardinal serves under the pope.

PRIEST: a person who serves God and may also be the minister of a church

SEMINARY: a school for future priests